God, Man
&
Mrs Thatcher

Jonathan
RABAN

God, Man
&
Mrs Thatcher

Chatto & Windus
LONDON

Published in 1989 by
Chatto & Windus Ltd
30 Bedford Square
London WC1B 3SG

A CIP catalogue record for this book is available from the British Library

ISBN 0 7011 3470 4

Copyright © Jonathan Raban 1989

Photoset by Rowland Phototypesetting Ltd
Bury St Edmunds, Suffolk
Printed in Great Britain by
Redwood Burn Ltd, Trowbridge, Wiltshire

'Is there such a thing as Mrs Thatcher?'
— Francis, aged 5

Preface

MUCH THE most strikingly original quality possessed by Mrs Thatcher is her integrity. I use the word not – or at least not exclusively – in its secondary sense, of having the character of uncorrupted virtue, but in its primary one, defined by the *OED* as 'the condition of having no part or element wanting; unbroken state; material wholeness, completeness, entirety'. Her physical bearing and appearance, her dress, hair, voice, style of thought and turns of phrase are more impressively all-of-a-piece than those of any British politician in recent history, Churchill not excepted. 'Thatcherism' is vested squarely in the person of Margaret Thatcher.

Like any practical politician, she has altered course to suit the changing weather. 'The lady's not for turning' has been a catchphrase, but she has swerved, sometimes violently, on policies and doctrines as central to her basic platform as adherence to strict monetarism, the balance between manufacturing and service industries and the promise to radically lower the level of public expenditure. Yet her integrity has been such that each new line has sounded just as authentically 'Thatcherite' as the one it has modified or supplanted.

She has an extraordinary gift for making ghost-written words her own. To read Jefferson's draft of the Declaration of Independence, Abraham Lincoln's Gettysburg Address, or the transcript of one of Churchill's wartime broadcasts is to have privileged access to the inside of one man's mind in its search for suitably expressive language. But the modern political speech tends to be an industrially manufactured product. In the United States, things are so far gone that the speechwriter has emerged as a dramatist in his own right. When George Bush accepted the Republican nomination in New Orleans in 1988, he made an unusually successful speech which hinged on his personal memories of flying combat missions in World War 2. The speechwriter was Peggy Noonan, who was herself born after the end of that war. Asked for her opinion of Bush's performance, Ms Noonan said it was just fine, marred only by one or two unscheduled departures from her original text; the best advice she could give the Vice-President was to stick to the words he was given in future, and not to experiment with hazardous ad-libbery.

Mrs Thatcher, though, is famous among contemporary politicians for the thoroughness with which she vets her scripts. Patrick Cosgrave and others have documented the amount of work that goes into the creation of a final Thatcher text – the drafts sent back, with a wigging, to their authors, the crossings-out and tearings-up, the generous application of Margaret Thatcher's own pen.

Her speech to the Assembly of the Church of Scotland in May 1988 was a special case. It was both extraordinarily wide-ranging, in its treatment of issues of Church and State, social and economic policy, the meaning of democracy itself, and extraordinarily personal, bedded firmly down in anecdotes from Mrs Thatcher's childhood and informed throughout by her theological upbringing in the Methodist Church.

Other people will undoubtedly have had a hand in the speech's drafting, but every page is stamped with phrases peculiar to Mrs Thatcher and with her own syntactical oddities. If one compares the text of the speech with a radio interview she gave two months later on *The Jimmy Young Programme* (which is as near as most ordinary citizens can come to hearing the Prime Minister talking in an unbuttoned and unscripted mood), there is a remarkable linguistic consistency between the two. The language of Mrs Thatcher, in Parliament, on the stump and in conversation, is distinct, recognisable, uniform in tone. It has integrity.

She has been criticised for being a poor orator, for the artificially lowered timbre of her voice, for her stilted way of talking, even in private. Intimate admirers have commented on her air of bringing a lectern, complete with a tumbler of iced water, into the drawing room. Yet Mrs Thatcher's rather strained and difficult relationship with the English language has served her purposes very well.

In oratory, as in economics, she is an iconoclast. That she would never rise to Macmillan's figurative 'wind of change . . .', or even to Harold Wilson's 'white heat of the technological revolution . . .', stems not so much from linguistic inability as from conviction. She is against abstractions. She distrusts the loose morals of metaphor. She is resolutely for the penny-plain rather than the tuppence-coloured. She is fond of homely clichés, often resurrecting expressions that have become antique with over-usage, like 'nitty-gritty', 'airy-fairy', 'moaning Minnies'. She can use the most hackneyed phrase as if she had minted it that morning.

Her language is insistently, aggressively, de-motic. Just as her Cabinets have contained fewer landowners, and fewer people with titles, than the Cabinets of any previous administration, Labour or Conservative, so her speeches are notably free of the aristocratic airs and graces of the traditional Establishment. She wears her bargain-basement language like a badge of virtue.

Politicians often complain that their speeches never receive as much careful analysis as they deserve. Texts are milked to make a single headline.

4

TV cameras are switched on only at the moment when the speaker arrives at the sentence of his script which the news editor, hours before the actual performance, has selected as a suitably juicy item for his evening bulletin. The details, the arguments, the complex internal logic of the speech don't get reported or explored. The sound bite rules.

This essay is meant as a gesture of rectification. My own training has been as a literary critic, not as a political commentator, and I've spent a lot of time trying to understand what texts mean – reading between the lines, listening for undertones and ironies, chasing up key words and images. The first-year student of literature is weaned on the idea that the meaning of a literary text is likely to reside as much in what is left unsaid, or accidentally let slip, or said in a significantly clumsy way, as in what is clearly stated. I've tried to read Mrs Thatcher's address to the Church of Scotland as if it had the resonance and density of a poem – which, in a way, it does.

Text of a speech
given by The Prime Minister
The Rt Hon Margaret Thatcher FRS MP
to the General Assembly of
The Church of Scotland
in Edinburgh
on
Saturday 21 May 1988

Press Office
Prime Minister's Office
10 Downing Street
Whitehall
London SW1

INTRODUCTION

Moderator and Members of the Assembly:

I am greatly honoured to have been invited to attend the opening of this 1988 General Assembly of the Church of Scotland; and I am deeply grateful that you have now asked me to address you.

I am very much aware of the historical continuity extending over four centuries, during which the position of the Church of Scotland has been recognised in constitutional law and confirmed by successive Sovereigns. It sprang from the independence of mind and rigour of thought that have always been such powerful characteristics of the Scottish people. It has remained close to its roots and has inspired a commitment to service from *all* people.

I am therefore very sensible of the important influence which the Church of Scotland exercises in the life of the whole nation, both at the spiritual level and through the extensive caring services which are provided by your Church's department of social responsibility.

CHRISTIANITY – SPIRITUAL AND SOCIAL

Perhaps it would be best if I began by speaking personally as a Christian, as well as a politician, about the way I see things. Reading recently I came across the starkly simple phrase: 'Christianity is about spiritual redemption, not social reform'.

Sometimes the debate on these matters has become too polarised and given the impression that the two are quite separate.

Most Christians would regard it as their personal Christian duty to help their fellow men and women. They would regard the lives of children a precious trust. These duties come not from any secular legislation passed by Parliament, but from being a Christian.

But there are a number of people who are not Christians who would also accept those responsibilities. What then are the distinctive marks of Christianity?

They stem not from the social but from the spiritual side of our lives. I would identify three beliefs in particular:

First, that from the beginning man has been endowed by God with the fundamental right to choose between good and evil.

Second, that we were made in God's own image and therefore we are expected to use all our *own* power of thought and judgement in exercising that choice; and further, if we open our hearts to God, He has promised to work within us.

And third, that Our Lord Jesus Christ The Son of God, when faced with His terrible choice and lonely vigil *chose* to lay down His life that our sins may be forgiven. I remember very well a sermon on an Armistice Sunday when our Preacher said

'No one took away the life of Jesus, He chose to lay it down'.

I think back to many discussions in my early life when we all agreed that if you try to take the fruits of Christianity without its roots, the fruits will wither. And they will not come again unless you nurture the roots.

But we must not profess the Christian faith and go to Church simply because we want social reforms and benefits or a better standard of behaviour – but because we accept the sanctity of life, the responsibility that comes with freedom and the supreme sacrifice of Christ expressed so well in the hymn:

> 'When I survey the wondrous Cross
> On which the Prince of glory died,
> My richest gain I count but loss,
> And pour contempt on all my pride.'

BIBLE PRINCIPLES – RELEVANCE TO POLITICAL LIFE

May I also say a few words about my personal belief in the relevance of Christianity to public policy – to the things that are Caesar's?

The Old Testament lays down in Exodus the Ten Commandments as given to Moses, the injunction in Leviticus to love our neighbour as ourselves and generally the importance of observing a strict code of law. The New Testament is a record of the Incarnation, the teachings of Christ and the establishment of the Kingdom of God. Again we have the emphasis on loving our neighbour as ourselves and to 'Do-as-you-would-be-done-by'.

I believe that by taking together these key elements from the Old and New Testaments, we gain:
  a view of the universe,
  a proper attitude to work,
  and principles to shape economic and social life.

We are told we must work and use our talents to create wealth. 'If a man will not work he shall not eat' wrote St Paul to the Thessalonians. Indeed, abundance rather than poverty has a legitimacy which derives from the very nature of Creation.

Nevertheless, the Tenth Commandment – Thou shalt not covet – recognises that making money and owning things could become selfish activities. But it is not the creation of wealth that is wrong but love of money for its own sake. The spiritual dimension comes in deciding what one does with the wealth. How could we respond to the many calls for help, or invest for the future, or support the wonderful artists and craftsmen whose work also glorifies God, unless we had first worked hard and used our talents to create the necessary wealth? And remember the woman with the alabaster jar of ointment.

I confess that I always had difficulty with interpreting the Biblical precept to love our neighbours 'as ourselves' until I read some of the words of C. S. Lewis. He pointed out that we don't exactly love *ourselves* when we fall below the standards and beliefs we have accepted. Indeed we might even *hate* ourselves for some unworthy deed.

POLITICAL ACTION AND PERSONAL RESPONSIBILITIES

None of this, of course, tells us exactly what kind of political and social institutions we should have. On this point, Christians will very often genuinely disagree, though it is a mark of Christian manners that they will do so with courtesy and mutual respect. What is certain, however, is that any set of social and economic arrangements which is not founded on the acceptance of individual responsibility will do nothing but harm. We are all responsible for our own actions. We cannot blame society if we disobey the law. We simply cannot delegate the exercise of mercy and generosity to others. The politicians and other secular powers should strive by their measures to bring out the good in people and to fight down the bad: but they can't create the one or abolish the other. They can only see that the laws encourage the *best* instincts and convictions of the people, instincts and convictions which I am convinced are far more deeply rooted than is often supposed.

Nowhere is this more evident than the basic ties of the family which are at the heart of our society and are the very nursery of civic virtue.

It is on the family that we in government build our own policies for welfare, education and care.

You recall that Timothy was warned by St Paul that anyone who neglects to provide for his own house (meaning his own family) has disowned the faith and is 'worse than an infidel'.

We must recognise that modern society is infinitely more complex than that of Biblical times and of course new occasions teach new duties. In our generation, the only way we can ensure that no-one is left without sustenance, help or opportunity, is to have laws to provide for health and education, pensions for the elderly, succour for the sick and disabled.

But intervention by the State must never become so great that it effectively removes personal responsibility. The same applies to taxation for while you and I would work extremely hard whatever the circumstances, there are undoubtedly some who would not unless the incentive was there. And we need *their* efforts too.

RELIGIOUS EDUCATION

Moderator, recently there have been great debates about religious education. I believe strongly that politicians must see that religious education has a proper place in the school curriculum.

In Scotland as in England there is an historic connection expressed in our laws between Church and State. The two connections are of a somewhat different kind, but the arrangements in both countries are designed to give symbolic expression to the same crucial truth – that the Christian religion – which, of course, embodies many of the great spiritual and moral truths of Judaism – is a fundamental part of our national heritage. I believe it is the wish of the overwhelming majority of people that this heritage should be preserved and fostered. For centuries it has been our very life blood. Indeed we are a nation whose ideals are founded on the Bible.

Also, it is quite impossible to understand our history or literature without grasping this fact. *That* is the strong practical case for ensuring that children at school are given adequate instruction in the part which the Judaic–Christian tradition has played in moulding our laws, manners and institutions. How can you make sense of Shakespeare and Sir Walter Scott, or of the constitutional conflicts of the 17th century in both Scotland and England, without some such fundamental knowledge?

But I go further than this. The truths of the Judaic–Christian tradition are infinitely precious, not only, as I believe, because they are true, but also because they provide the moral impulse which alone can lead to that peace, in the true meaning of the word, for which we all long.

TOLERANCE

To assert absolute moral values is not to claim perfection for ourselves. No true Christian could do that. What is more, one of the great principles of our Judaic–Christian inheritance is tolerance.

People with other faiths and cultures have always been welcomed in our land, assured of equality under the law, of proper respect and of open friendship.

There is absolutely nothing incompatible between this and our desire to maintain the essence of our own identity. There is no place for racial or religious intolerance in our creed.

CHRISTIANS AND DEMOCRACY

When Abraham Lincoln spoke in his famous Gettysburg speech of 1863 of 'government of the people, by the people, and for the people', he gave the world a neat definition of democracy which has since been widely and enthusiastically adopted. But what he enunciated as a form of government was not in itself especially Christian, for nowhere in the Bible is the word democracy mentioned. Ideally, when Christians meet, as Christians, to take counsel together their purpose is not (or should not be) to ascertain what is the mind of the majority but what is the mind of the Holy Spirit – something which may be quite different.

Nevertheless I am an enthusiast for democracy. And I take that position, not because I believe majority opinion is inevitably right or true, indeed no majority can take away God-given human rights. But because I believe it most effectively safeguards the value of the individual, and, more than any other system, restrains the abuse of power by the few. And that *is* a Christian concept.

But there is little hope for democracy if the hearts of men and women in democratic societies cannot be touched by a call to something greater than themselves. Political structures, state institutions, collective ideals are not enough. *We* Parliamentarians can legislate for the rule of *law*. *You* the Church can teach the life of faith.

CONCLUSION

For, when all is said and done, a politician's role is a humble one. I always think that the whole debate about the Church and the State has never yielded anything comparable in insight to that beautiful hymn 'I vow to thee my country'. It begins with a triumphant assertion of what might be described as secular patriotism, a noble thing indeed in a country like ours:

'I vow to thee my country all earthly things above;
entire, whole and perfect the service of my love'.

It goes on to speak of 'another country I heard of long ago' whose King cannot be seen and whose armies cannot be counted, but 'soul by soul and silently her shining bounds increase'. Not group by

19

group or party by party or even church by church
– but soul by soul and each one counts.

That, members of the Assembly, is the country
which you chiefly serve. You fight your cause under
the banner of an historic church. Your success
matters greatly – as much to the temporal as to the
spiritual welfare of the nation.

God, Man & Mrs Thatcher

I AM GREATLY honoured . . . and I am deeply grateful. For the Prime Minister this was a tricky Away fixture. Scotland was the most solidly anti-Tory region in the United Kingdom. Many of her audience were plainly listening to her on sufferance. Furthermore, her real quarrel was with the bishops of the Church of England – never since the English Revolution had there been such open acrimony between the government and the established church south of the border. Yet rather than bearding the lions of York and Canterbury in their dens, Margaret Thatcher chose to make her pitch on Church and State to the Scottish Calvinists in Edinburgh. She is now an Anglican churchgoer, but all her training in the hard school of the Finkin Street Methodist Church at Grantham must have made Edinburgh seem like a theological homecoming. The Calvinists were people she could speak to in the strict, Nonconformist, evangelical terms that come most easily to her.

Independence of mind . . . rigour of thought. Her account of the foundation of the Church of Scotland has a curious doubleness to it, as if, in describing the institution, she was also sketching a thumbnail self-portrait. That 'independence of mind' was libertarian, anti-establishment, democratic. In Calvin's lifetime, and to Calvin's consternation, John Knox was preaching the right of the people to overthrow 'false princes'. One remembers Knox's famous exchanges with his Queen – exchanges that have a familiar ring to anyone who believes the gossip about Mrs Thatcher's audiences with our present monarch:

Knox Yea Madam, I offer myself further to prove that the Church of Rome is declined, and more than five hundred years hath declined, from the purity of that religion which the Apostles taught and planted.

Mary My conscience is not so.

Knox Conscience, Madam, requires knowledge: and I fear that right knowledge ye have none.

Mary But I have both heard and read.

Knox So Madam, did the Jews that crucified Jesus Christ read both the Law and the Prophets . . .

Knox's libertarian politics went hand in hand with 'rigour' – severity, strictness, conformity – in doctrine and morality. He followed Calvin's watchwords of will-power, discipline and order. Robert Louis Stevenson wrote of Knox:

Like many men, and many Scotchmen, he saw the world and his own heart, not so much under any very steady, equable light, as by extreme flashes of passion, true for the moment, but not true in the long run. There does seem to me to be something of this traceable in the Reformer's utterances: precipitation and repentance, hardy speech and action somewhat circumspect, a strong tendency to see himself in a heroic light and to place a ready belief in the disposition of the moment. Withal he had considerable confidence in himself, and in the uprightness of his own disciplined emotions, underlying much sincere aspiration after spiritual humility.

How could Thatcher fail to see in the character of John Knox the ghostly outline of a kindred spirit?

. . . *historical continuity . . . it has remained close to its roots* . . . Praising Knox's church, Mrs Thatcher uses two of her most cherished words, 'history' and 'roots'. Her own break with the past has been radical to the point of being revolutionary, yet, like those scriptural annotators for whom every verse of the New Testament can be grounded in the foretext of the Old, she continually employs 'history' as the great licensing authority, to validate each new departure from historical practice. Her notions of what actually happened in history are often eccentric, sometimes downright ignorant – perhaps necessarily so, since no one who knew much about the Victorian period could possibly ascribe Margaret Thatcher's meaning to the term 'Victorian values'. At fonder moments (as later in this speech), she substitutes the phrase 'our heritage' for 'history' – and 'heritage' expresses her meaning far more accurately. For a heritage is something we have possession of after the death of its original owners, and we are free to use it as we choose. The fine Victorian mahogany commode, designed as a useful receptacle for excrement, now comes in handy as a cocktail cabinet; and so history-as-heritage simply offers a challenge to the ingenuity of its new owner. You can house the video and the guts of the stereo system inside it; have it painted with shepherds and shepherdesses; plant bonsai in its cracked ceramic bowl.

'Roots', though, are different. Where history is an infinitely malleable substance in Margaret Thatcher's language, 'roots' are intractable and particular, and it is the first mark of your integrity that you remain close to them. She has said 'One of my favourite quotations is: "That which thy father bequeathed thee, earn it anew, if thou wouldst possess it"' – and was talking not about history or national tradition but about Alfred Roberts and the grocer's shop. The Church of Scotland has kept faith with John Knox and Edinburgh just as Margaret Thatcher has kept faith with Alderman Roberts and Grantham. (There is, too, the strong implicit suggestion that the Church of England has *not* remained close to its roots – that Jenkins and Runcie have failed to keep faith with Hooker, Taylor, and the seventeenth century divines who shaped the spiritual doctrines of the C. of E.)

The little acreage in which Margaret Thatcher's own roots are planted is well worth the five-minute detour from the A1. The grocer's shop stands on the corner between Broad Street and North Parade. When I was there, someone had cashed in on its status as a national shrine by converting it into the Premier Restaurant, with a chi-chi mock-up of a 1930s corner shop in the lobby. The building surprised me by its relative grandeur. I had known that Margaret Thatcher had grown up in a house without a bathroom and with an outdoor lavatory, and had expected something altogether pokier than these three storeys of weathered red-brick, standing on the street corner of what looks like a demonstrator's model of British society. For North Parade is solidly, Georgianly, genteel, with its golden-section windows and moulded porticos; it is sturdy, tidy, tall, unimpeachably mercantile and middle class. Broad Street, though, which is also a short street, of fifty yards or less, connects the uppish world of North Parade with the low, two-storey terraces of Albion Street and New Street. The Robertses' shop looks modestly up to North Parade

25

and rather proudly down on Albion Street. Diagonally across from the shop, on the far side of North Parade, is the Blue Bull public house; immediately behind it stands the Primitive Methodist Chapel (1886), a narrow-windowed, slate-roofed building that looks like the Robertses' rear-wheel-drive engine. Opposite the shop is the North Parade Roman Catholic Church, while on the corner of Albion and New Streets, in the working class terraces, is the Little Gonerby Church of England Infants' School. A sketchmap may be useful:

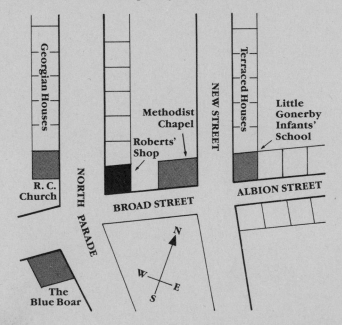

Standing on the corner, you can see at a glance who's up, who's down, who gets tick and who is sternly told not to ask for credit as a refusal may offend. Church, chapel and pub, town house and terrace, North and South, East and West – the social cartography of this bit of Grantham is laid out with diagrammatic plainness.

The Sabbatarian regime of the Roberts household was strict. Alfred Roberts was an itinerant lay preacher; the family walked to the Finkin Street church – a mile away from the shop – three times each Sunday. Reading and games were forbidden on the Lord's Day. When Margaret Roberts introduced Mr Denis Thatcher to her parents, he is said to have been – understandably – awed by the family's Nonconformist zealotry.

... *inspired a commitment to service from* all *people* ... The emphasis is Mrs Thatcher's, and it flies at once boldly, and a shade wistfully, in the face of the facts. Events at Ibrox Park whenever Rangers meet Celtic bear bloody witness to the fact that the Church of Scotland is only one sect among several in the country. Yet the dream of universal conversion dies hard among evangelists. In 1979, Mrs Thatcher told Kenneth Harris, 'You can only get other people in tune with you by being a little evangelical about it'; in 1988, talking on *The Jimmy Young Programme*, she said of 'Thatcherism', 'It's because it strikes a chord in the hearts and minds of men and women that they say yes and believe it'. To be a 'Thatcherite' is, in Margaret Thatcher's

27

own terms, to experience an epiphany, to undergo a religious transfiguration. Addressing the Church of Scotland, a body uncannily like herself in its independence, rigour, rootedness and evangelical fervour, she credited the Presbyterians with having conquered a whole nation with their faith. It was the highest compliment she could pay them. She was telling the Church of Scotland that it had achieved exactly what she dreams of accomplishing herself.

I am therefore very sensible ... 'Sensible', in this sense, is 'now somewhat rare', says the *OED*, but it has the right ring of measured loftiness. It is a regal word, a solemnly judicial word; it is the ceremonial cloak behind which the dagger of political assertion is concealed. It introduces the central antithesis on which the speech devolves: *both at the spiritual level and through the extensive caring services* ... The division between the realms of Spiritual and Temporal is nicely incised by that 'both ... and ...'. The word 'level' (which might otherwise have been represented by 'side', 'aspect', or 'element') suggests a hierarchy, with spiritual things up on the top floor and the extensive caring services down on G.

The way I see things ... For Margaret Thatcher's view of this is decidedly not that of the Church of

Scotland, which sees its 'caring services' as an indissoluble constituent of its theology – as the Word embodied in practical action. There is more than a touch of Knoxian 'precipitation and repentance, hardy speech and action somewhat circumspect' in the Prime Minister's manner here as she endorses, then retracts, then reindorses the idea that 'Christianity is about spiritual redemption, not social reform'.

The starkly simple phrase is surely a warm recommendation in this Calvinist setting, where the stark and the simple are held in high moral regard. Yet no sooner has the starkly simple phrase been uttered than Mrs Thatcher is ducking out from under it. *Sometimes the debate on these matters has become too polarised* ... So it ought to be polarised, but not *too* polarised; just as *the impression that the two are quite separate* suggests that they are indeed separate, but not *quite* separate.

From here on in, as she wades deeper into the treacherous waters of Christian doctrine, she relies on her passion for qualified measurement and enumeration to keep her footing. Mrs Thatcher has a natural mistrust of ideas. She calls them 'concepts', and likes to disparage them as 'airy-fairy'. The idea of a federated Europe, for instance, is 'an airy-fairy concept'; so, more bewilderingly, is the idea of 'society' (which she has redefined as 'you and me and our next-door neighbour and everyone we

29

know in our town'). She is formidably at home with substances – with things that can be weighed and counted, sliced and wrapped in parcels.

Every biography of Mrs Thatcher has a touching paragraph about how the young Margaret Roberts used to help her parents in the shop, weighing sugar and butter on old-fashioned scales with brass weights. At Oxford she took a Second in Chemistry – the perfect subject for someone so wedded to the tangible. Chemistry is the least airy-fairy of disciplines, with its jars of crystals, scales, retorts and bunsen burners. In Kenneth Harris's 1988 biography, *Thatcher*, there is a photograph of her working as a research chemist in 1949 or 1950, either at British Xylonite in Manningtree or at J. Lyons & Co in Hammersmith. A pestle and mortar sit on the table in the foreground, along with a knife and a pair of scales in a glass case. In the background are shelf on shelf of stoppered bottles. The Prime Minister-to-be is leaning forward, her 'fierce and unrelenting glare' (the phrase is Julian Critchley's) sternly focused on the business of pouring something from a measuring-glass into a rather pretty vase containing another liquid, and stirring the mixture with a spatula. She might be controlling the money supply.

For the article of faith on which she rode to power in 1979 was based on a belief in quantifiable substance. Out of Milton Friedman, by Alfred

Sherman, rigorous monetarism had the appeal of a chemical formula. In M3, it had an analysable content, like H^2O or CO^2. The economy could be controlled with a tap and a measuring glass. Indeed, it was simpler than Chemistry. It was like selling a paper twist of castor sugar on Broad Street – a quarter pound exactly, not three-and-a-half or four-and-a-quarter ounces, and you could 'revive the philosophy and principles of a free society'.

So here she portions out, qualifies, enumerates and rings up the total on the till. *Most Christians* accept two duties – *to help their fellow men and women* and to care for their children as *a precious trust*. However, *a number of people who are not Christians* also love their children and help their friends. *Most* implies *not all*; *a number* suggests a substantially larger number of which it is only a measurable fraction.

This is alarming news. Many people, probably many millions, accept neither duty. Who are they, and where do they live? I rang an anthropologist to ask if he knew their names and whereabouts, but he was almost as much at a loss as I was. It was true, he said, that some tribes, when forcibly displaced from their traditional terrain and means of survival, had adopted some odd forms of social and family behaviour. The Ik, for instance, were supposed to have taken to pushing their grannies over high cliffs as a sport. In general, though, he could only state the obvious: that any society which failed to love and look after its children would rapidly cease to exist.

The distinctive marks of Christianity . . . stem not from the social but from the spiritual side of our lives (that bacon-slicing antithesis again). Where the Church of England lists thirty-nine essential articles of faith, Mrs Thatcher names three: the belief in the doctrine of Free-Will; in the divinely created sovereignty of individual conscience; and in the Crucifixion and Redemption as the exemplary, supreme act of choice. It is interesting to go back to the *Thirty Nine Articles of Religion* in order to check on what Mrs Thatcher has left out. Some of the most conspicuous omissions are: faith in the Trinity (Article 1), in the Resurrection and Ascension (Article 4), in Original Sin (Article 9), in Justification by Faith alone (Article 11), in Salvation (Article 17), and in the Sacraments (Article 25). Article 10, *Of Free-Will*, has an important qualification, not mentioned by Mrs Thatcher:

> The Condition of Man after the fall of *Adam*, is such, that he cannot turn and prepare himself by his own natural Strength and Good Works to Faith and calling upon God: wherefore we have no power to do good Works, pleasant and acceptable to God, without the Grace of God, by Christ preventing us, that we may have a Good Will, and working with us, when we have that Good Will.

32

The Three Articles of Mrs Thatcher are re-morselessly reductive. They boil down Christianity to provide a theological legitimation for the doctrine of the individual's *right to choose*. The word *choice* is hammered into each Article, and by Article 3 the meaning of the Crucifixion itself turns out to be that Christ was exercising His right to choose.

That phrase! It has been used by Margaret Thatcher so often before, in contexts so far removed from the theological, that an unseemly bathos attaches itself to it here. Christ dying on the Cross joins those folk who have exercised their right to choose – to buy their own council houses, to send their children to private schools, to occupy 'paybeds' in NHS-funded hospitals.

Yet something much more subtle is also going on in this passage, and it would be a mistake to see Mrs Thatcher as merely twisting Christian dogma into the shape of her own pet political maxim. She is not theologically naive. Her Articles are grounded in a long tradition of Christian reformism - a tradition extending from Luther, Zwingli, Calvin and Knox to John Wesley. The heart of Article 2 – the fulcrum point of this declaration of faith – is *use all our* own *power of thought and judgement*, with its ringing stress on the word *own*.

In the pre-Reformation Church, man (at least the individual layman) was not so dependent, so lonely, in the exercise of his *own* faculties. A huge apparatus

33

of mediating institutions had been erected to cushion the terrible relationship between one man and his God. These institutions justified the ways of Man to God at the same time as they justified the ways of God to Man. The papacy and its priesthood took over much of the responsibility for *thought and judgement*. The profitable industry which had grown up around the sale of papal indulgences, and whose excesses caused Luther to nail his Ninety-Five Theses to the door of the Castle Church in Wittenberg, formed another buffer-state between the individual and the Creator. Even in their private prayers, men and women addressed God through the intercessionary, Ombudsmanlike figure of the Virgin.

The whole thrust of the Reformation in its radical and libertarian form (in Calvinism and its subsequent offshoots) was to destroy this mediating apparatus. There were to be no buffer-states. Man was to stand naked before God, without benefit of intercession or priestcraft. The English Puritans who founded the colony of Massachusetts had a holy horror of stained glass windows, because they represented a vain attempt by Man to shield himself from God's gaze with placatory icons.

It is to this puritan and pietistic tradition that Mrs Thatcher appeals in her Articles – to Conscience as a peculiarly solitary responsibility. Like Calvin himself, she will have no truck with mediating institutions. On this, the record of her government

34

is both logical and exemplary, with its attacks on the Church, the BBC and the universities, on powerful agencies of local government like the GLC, and even (especially over South African sanctions) on the monarchy. She is passionately 'anti-statist' – yet every institution which has traditionally stood between the individual and central government has been either abolished or has come under heavy fire from her administration. If the Kingdom of Man is a shadowy reflection of the Kingdom of God, then Margaret Thatcher is a good Calvinist; for it is emerging as a fundamental principle of 'Thatcherism' that a man shall stand as nakedly before his Government as he does before his Maker.

In my early life . . . Margaret Thatcher always uses this phrase, or a close variant of it, when most people would say 'In my childhood', or 'When I was young'. It is a surprisingly old habit. When she was challenging Edward Heath for the leadership of the Conservative Party in 1975, she told her constituents in Finchley:

> You can forget all the nonsense about 'defence of privilege' – I had precious little 'privilege' *in my early years* – and the suggestion that all my supporters are reactionary right-wingers . . . (*emphases added*)

35

Yet to possess an *early life* is a privilege in itself, for it puts you in the company of those saints and historical figures whose *early lives* are chronicled for the edification of later generations. Stevenson said of Knox that he had 'a strong tendency to see himself in a heroic light', and so does Margaret Thatcher. It is by tokens like *my early life* that she reveals how she is inclined to think of herself in the historical third person, marked by Destiny from infancy as the instrument of a force greater than herself. When Norman St John Stevas was the licensed jester of the Thatcher court, he twitted her with nicknames like 'The Blessed Margaret' and 'The Immaculate Misconception'; during the Falklands war, Alexander Haig was impressed by the 'Messianic' view that she took of her own role in the affair. The phrasing and the tone of her 'men and women . . . say yes and believe it' line on *The Jimmy Young Programme* contrived to suggest that the Prime Minister was not so much the architect of a political programme as the founder of a holy creed. For the true Thatcherite, faith in the person of the founder is an essential article of belief, and the Prime Minister has a trick of manifesting herself as the Good Shepherd of Grantham.

. . . if you try to take the fruits of Christianity without its roots, the fruits will wither. And they will not come again unless you nurture the roots. It is a mystical conundrum, a paradoxical Truth gleaned from the

36

Prime Minister's *early life*. In the first sentence, you appear to have to eat the roots, an unpleasant business, like Dutch people having to eat tulip bulbs in the last days of German occupation; in the second, you merely need to keep them watered. That the grammar of the metaphor goes to pieces only serves to underline the sacred, paralogical status of *roots* in Mrs Thatcher's rhetoric. Whether they are her own roots, or those of Christianity (and the two may well be inseparable), *roots* are there to *remain close to*, to *take* (as in 'take communion') and to *nurture*. The question of how you do any of these things is left open. It is one of the few Impenetrable Mysteries in Mrs Thatcher's otherwise clear, practical and positivist theology.

. . . *the supreme sacrifice of Christ expressed so well in the hymn* . . . We are still in the realm of paradox here. For 'When I survey the wondrous Cross' does not *express* the *sacrifice of Christ*. It expresses, rather, the humility and gratitude of the Cross's surveyor – and expresses them in terms that one would have thought were unhelpful to the argument in hand. Contemplation of the Cross causes the hymn-writer to count his richest gain as loss, and leads him, in the next stanza, to a devout renunciation of luxury goods:

> All the vain things that charm me most
> I sacrifice them to His Blood.

*

37

... *The things that are Caesar's* ... When the chief priests and scribes in Jerusalem sent their spies to Christ, in an attempt to trick him into an insurrectionist statement, his 'Render unto Caesar' reply had them foxed. 'They could not take hold of his words before the people: and they marvelled at his answer, and held their peace.' The situation here is interestingly different. Margaret Thatcher, as civil ruler, has entered the house of the chief priests and scribes, the ecclesiastical establishment. She is Caesar in person, and she is laying down a warning claim to her own territory.

Her breezy synopsis of the essential content of both the Old and the New Testaments leads her to another of her reductive lists-of-three. *A view of the universe*, put like this, without further elaboration, sounds merely like an attractive and desirable amenity, like a view of the sea. *A proper attitude to work* is more like it. *Proper* is one of Mrs Thatcher's keywords. It represents the exact quarter-pound measure, neither too much nor too little; it corresponds with the *OED*'s *III, 2* definition, *In conformity with the demands or usages of society; decent, decorous, respectable, 'correct'*. It's an odd word to use in this context, since it implies that we, as a society, already know what is *proper* without needing to be taught it. *We* (by definition, otherwise we would not be using the word) know what is *proper*; but *they* may

38

not. So the Bible teaches *them* what is *the proper attitude to work.*

Principles to shape economic and social life spawns four more apophthegms, though this time they are scattered, somewhat secretively, through the ensuing text. The four are: that *we must work and use our talents to create wealth*; that we must observe the Tenth Commandment, *Thou shalt not covet*; that we must distribute our wealth, not equitably, but well; and that we must correctly interpret *the Biblical precept to love our neighbours 'as ourselves'.*

... *talents to create wealth* ... is a constructive misunderstanding of the nature of parable. In the parables, Christ habitually uses unlikely secular vehicles to convey complex moral ideas, and the Parable of the Talents is a fine example of His style at its most teasingly playful and paradoxical. The rich man who leaves money for his servants to invest (or bury in the garden) is a deliberately improbable stand-in for God. The Parable of the Talents teaches man to act positively in the world, to try to make the most of what he is given, to increase his inheritance; here Mrs Thatcher appears to regard it simply as a divine sanction for the bond-broker and the arbitrageur.

In fact *wealth* is a word that is always hedged about with heavy caveats by Biblical authors. In Deuteronomy 8, *wealth* is given to man by God for one purpose only: 'The Lord thy God ... giveth thee power to get wealth, that he may establish his covenant'. In II Chronicles 1, Solomon is granted *wealth* (as well as wisdom) only because he did not seek it. Job associates wealth with the wicked: 'Wherefore do the wicked live? . . . They spend their days in wealth, and in a moment go down to the grave'. Proverbs warn that 'The rich man's wealth is his strong city, and as an high wall in his own conceit'. Mrs Thatcher's favourite Biblical author, St Paul, writes to the Corinthians: 'Let no man seek his own, but every man another's wealth'.

But the stuff clearly has its uses. 'Mighty men of wealth' – the James Goldsmiths and Rupert Murdochs of their day – show up on two occasions in the Old Testament. In Ruth, Ruth herself is employed, on generous terms, by Boaz, a mighty man of wealth, and later marries him. Less romantically, mighty men of wealth are used in II Kings 15 as a convenient tax base for defence expenditure.

In general, wealth is conceived as a matter of luck and grace, as an unexpected bounty granted by God to those, like Solomon, who haven't pursued it as an end. Searching for a text to back up Margaret Thatcher's interpretation of the Bible, the nearest I could find was Proverbs 13, v. 11: 'Wealth gotten by vanity shall be diminished: but he that gathereth by labour shall increase'. She should, however, be reminded by Proverbs 22, v. 1: 'A good name is rather to be chosen than riches'.

If a man will not work he shall not eat ... After the speech had been delivered, it was this sentence that was remembered more than any other. It was blazoned on newspaper headlines, and I have heard Mrs Thatcher's address described as 'Oh, you mean the if-a-man-will-not-work-he-shall-not-eat speech?' It is true that in the last chapter of Paul's second epistle to the Thessalonians he comes down very toughly on Thessalonian laziness. He reminds his readers that he himself worked for his bread when he was visiting Salonica, and observes that 'there are some which walk among you disorderly, working not at all, but are busybodies'. These Greek welfare-scroungers clearly needed the smack of firm government.

First century Salonica, though, was rather a special case. It stood at the head of the Gulf of Thermaikos and was much the largest and safest natural harbour in the region. It was backed by a fertile plain watered by four big rivers, which narrowed to the famously beautiful Vale of Tempe. With its trade and shipping, its fishing and farming, it was one of the richest places in the world, with more than its fair share of Lotus-eaters. It would have been a very lazy Thessalonian indeed who failed to earn his daily crust there, in a society with full employment and jobs for the taking (even Paul, a tourist, had found work during his stay in Salonica).

Abundance rather than poverty has a legitimacy which derives from the very nature of Creation. This is both a *non-sequitur* and a false antithesis. Paul has, after all, been writing of work, not as a means of gaining wealth, but as the means by which the easy-living Thessalonians should 'eat their own bread'. He is referring back to the third chapter of the Book of Genesis, where God lists the punishments he will inflict on Adam for eating of the Tree of Knowledge. Work is one of them. 'In the sweat of thy face shalt thou eat bread till thou return unto the ground.' Neither Adam nor the Thessalonians are offered *abundance*; they are both told to sweat for mere sufficiency. *Abundance* is not the Biblical alternative to *poverty*: sufficiency is.

. . . making money and owning things could become selfish activities . . . Mrs Thatcher likes to get down to what she calls 'the nitty-gritty', and this Sunday School gloss on the Tenth Commandment is a nice example of the way she gets down to it. If one remembers her audience – of doctors of divinity, elders and presbyters – one can only admire the extraordinary fearlessness of her manner, as she lets them know what's what in language more usually suited to the instruction of five-year-olds.

It is exactly this manner that makes her beloved by so many people. *She* is not afraid to go among intellectuals, divines, the lah-di-dah classes with airy-fairy ideas, and get down to brass tacks with them in the sort of terms that you would use if your only regular reading was the *Express*. She cuts fancy folk down to size, and there is a heart-warming glee to be had at the sight of their discomfiture at the hands of 'Maggie'.

. . . deciding what one does with the wealth . . . Distribution of wealth earns another triad, and it is a strange list. Considered as a budget for national expenditure, it is a lot more radical than anything proposed so far by Mrs Thatcher's Chancellors of the Exchequer.

. . . respond to the many calls for help . . . The sick, the elderly, the jobless, the inadequately housed and inadequately paid are lumped in with the victims of foreign floods and earthquakes. *Calls for help* suggest emergencies; and all provisions for health and social welfare are here conceived as generous responses to particular emergencies.

. . . invest for the future . . . Education, general R. & D. and defence spending all appear to come under this heading.

. . . support the wonderful artists and craftsmen whose work also glorifies God . . . This is both much the longest and the most enthusiastic of the three, and it is a stirring vision. One imagines that Margaret Thatcher is thinking in vaguely Florentine terms – of Giotto at his drawing board, sketching the outlines of the Campanile, of Ghiberti carving the Door of Paradise for the Baptistry, of Michelangelo,

43

grubby with stone dust, chiselling the features of his *Pietà*, of Donatello sculpting *The Descent from the Cross* in exquisite relief for the church of San Lorenzo, while, in another century and another place, Handel, after breakfast, is to be found humming the preliminary bars of his *Messiah*.

But Mrs Thatcher has a problem with her audience here. In the early seventeenth century, the Presbyterians laid down an ordinance that walls of churches in Scotland must be bare and white-washed. John Knox, in Stevenson's characteris-ation, was famous for his zeal in 'breaking beautiful carved work in abbeys and cathedrals that had long smoked themselves out and were no more than sorry ruins'. Church music, like church painting and church craftsmanship, was outlawed. In Aberdeen in 1574, an order went out demanding that 'the organs, with all expeditioun, be removit out of the kirk'. In Edinburgh in 1988, I was talking with the former curator of a Scottish art gallery, who remarked that the Church of Scotland had been 'the chief blight' on the development of the arts in Scotland.

Perhaps Mrs Thatcher's own passion for the arts had overriden her sense of what was politic in a Calvinist context, for this is crusading talk. The idea that a third of the national wealth should be lavished on *wonderful artists and craftsmen* must have

44

electrified members of the Arts Council when they read it in their newspapers the next day.

There have been a few scattered hints of this passion. As a schoolgirl she used to give public recitations from Kipling and Palgrave's *Golden Treasury*. At Oxford, she sang in the Balliol-Somerville choir, and Kenneth Harris says that 'a shared liking for music' was an important part of the courtship of Margaret Roberts and Denis Thatcher. Her taste in painting is on record in the pages of *Hansard*, for in October 1987 she was required to give a written reply to a Member's question asking what paintings, engravings and photographs she had requisitioned for the walls of 10, Downing Street.

The list, which runs to five *Hansard* columns, is an unusual one for a serious devotee of painting. There are the statutory political portraits (including a Van Dyck print of Cromwell), landscapes by Turner and members of the Norwich School, marine pictures (two by William Van De Velde II), a surprisingly large collection of prints of military encampments. Mrs Thatcher's reverence for Kipling is reflected by a portrait of him by Sir Edward Burne-Jones. Her Oxford days are memorialised by many views of Oxford and its colleges. Cornwall (where she spends her summer holidays) is similarly honoured. She has an eighteenth century map of the Eastern Approaches to the Falkland

45

Islands. Two Gilmans and a Sickert suggest a possible, though somewhat faint, affection for the Camden Town school. 'Modern art' is represented by one repro Van Gogh (*Basket of Fruit with Blue Gloves*) and one repro Paul Klee (*Fish Magic*). From the Photographers Gallery, she borrowed on extended loan six Cibachrome landscapes in colour taken by Paul Wakefield. The list hardly suggests an informed or keen artistic taste. Perusal of it only makes her extravagant remarks about *wonderful artists and craftsmen* sound doubly mystifying.

And remember the woman with the alabaster jar of ointment . . . The alabaster jar (or 'box') contained oil of spikenard, an atrociously expensive aromatic substance, which this impulsive (and rich) woman emptied over Christ's head. The disciples remonstrated with her, saying that she could have sold the perfume for 'more than three hundred pence' and given the money to the poor. Christ said (St Mark 14, vv. 5–6):

> Let her alone; why trouble ye her? she hath wrought a good work on me. For ye have the poor with you always, and whensoever ye will ye may do them good: but me ye have not always.

So giving lavish presents may be not only more fun, but also more theologically sound, than pouring money down the bottomless drain of health and social welfare. Mrs Thatcher's knowing reminder is an oddly skittish way of poking the Presbyterians in the ribs.

Some of the words of C. S. Lewis ... Here too she is striking a pointedly un-Nonconformist note. Patrick Cosgrave, in his 1978 biography of Mrs Thatcher, describes her spare-time reading when she was a student at Somerville:

> She read widely in religion ... and settled very largely for the works of C. S. Lewis as her favourite. Thus began a move away from the Methodism of her childhood. 'I gradually went higher and higher,' she explains of the process by which she shifted slowly from a fundamentalist to a sacerdotal outlook.

However, even after her conversion to *Screwtape*, she continued to attend a student Methodist group. The business about going 'higher and higher' is most curious, since the whole cast of Mrs Thatcher's mind seems so consistently fundamentalist in its approach to everything from the economy to the Word. There is a possible clue in the way she has departed from Calvinist rigour in this section of her address, to proclaim herself in favour of Art and expensive perfume. Oxford, even if it didn't change the mental habits acquired at the Finkin Street church, clearly opened her eyes to the Good

47

Things of Life. The word 'higher' may have more to do with Society than with churchmanship.

... we don't exactly love ourselves when we fall below the standards and beliefs we have accepted. Indeed we might even hate *ourselves for some unworthy deed.* This is an ingenious loophole in *the precept to love our neighbours 'as ourselves'.* For if we don't exactly love — and might even hate — ourselves when we lapse from our own agreed standards of behaviour, how can we be under any serious compulsion to love other people who lapse from those same standards? *We* keep a good step; *we* refrain from playing loud music after 10.30 pm; *we* put our rubbish out in sealed black garbage bags. If the neighbours are slovenly, deafen us with Reggae in the small hours and chuck their chicken-bones into the street, here is a neat theological justification for loathing them. The traditional formulation used to be 'Hate the sin, but love the sinner'. Margaret Thatcher here revises it to something very close to 'Hate the sinner when his behaviour falls below the standards that you have set yourself', a proposition that would take a mighty broad church to accommodate it.

... On this point, Christians will very often genuinely disagree, though it is a mark of Christian manners that they will do so with courtesy and mutual respect. How stiff and unbending those courteous and mutually

48

respectful Christians sound, as they agree to differ. There's no suggestion that they have anything to gain from arguing with each other, that they might be persuaded to change or compromise their positions in debate. In Margaret Thatcher's rhetoric it is a clear sign of weakness to allow one's convictions to be shaken or diluted by anyone else's ideas.

Before she took office as Prime Minister in 1979, she told Kenneth Harris:

> I've got to have a Cabinet with equal unity of purpose and a sense of dedication to it. It must be a Cabinet that works on something much more than pragmatism or consensus. It must be a 'conviction' Government . . . We've got to go in an agreed and clear direction. As Prime Minister I couldn't waste time having any internal arguments.

That 'arguments' in Cabinet are 'a waste of time' is a chillingly original notion. As Walter Bagehot's *The English Constitution* makes plain, Cabinet is the supreme forum of British government. The secrecy of its meetings, together with the principle of collective responsibility for its decisions, were designed to liberate arguments within it, to allow Cabinet members the maximum freedom of debate behind closed doors. An idea is debatable by definition. A conviction ('a settled persuasion', *OED*) is not.

So the Christians, locked in frigid if polite

49

disagreement, are held up as an example of what happens when people have separate convictions. They would not qualify, in Margaret Thatcher's terms, for Cabinet membership. A Cabinet should be a committee in which everyone's settled persuasion is the same.

In the next sentence of her address, the whole theory of collective responsibility takes a savage knock:

> *Any set of social and economic arrangements which is not founded on the acceptance of individual responsibility will do nothing but harm.*

Does this apply to Cabinets too?

Certainly we are back to a soundly fundamentalist vision of man here, and to a relaunch of the attack on mediating institutions, whose nub is *We simply cannot delegate the exercise of mercy and generosity to others*; a statement worth pondering. *Delegate* here is used as if it meant to shrug off onto someone else's shoulders, or to wash one's hands of. In ordinary usage, to delegate means to commission or trust someone as an agent acting on your behalf; and a delegate is usually likely to do the job more professionally, more articulately, more effectively, than you'd do it yourself.

The individual delegates to government the exercise of many things: a defence policy founded on the narrow doctrine of individual responsibility would lead to a nation of minutemen; to each householder his own fowling-piece, and hang the MoD. Posses of neighbourhood vigilantes would supplant the police force, and the improvised society of the frontier would be held up as a moral ideal.

So it is only in the exercise of *mercy and generosity* that delegation and collectivism are to be deplored. This is perfectly just. 'Mercy', after all, is:

Forbearance and compassion shown by one person to another who is in his power *and who has no claim to receive kindness*.
(Italics added)

To delegate such a personal, and gratuitous, power would look suspiciously like resurrecting the industry of papal indulgences. Yet if the statement is so unexceptionable, so logically obvious, why does it need to be delivered with such rhetorical force? Surely it cannot mean that supplying for the needs of the poor and unemployed in a complex industrial society is forbearance and compassion shown to people who have no claim to receive kindness? Surely not.

. . . *to bring out the good in people and to fight down the bad* . . . Bringing out the good is something normally done to other people, by teachers, for instance; fighting down the bad is something

51

normally done to oneself, as when one fights down nausea, pride, panic. It is a revealing confusion of phrase, for in Margaret Thatcher's language control of the body and control of society are so closely identified with each other that sometimes, as here, they merge into one. As the anthropologist, Mary Douglas, has shown in *Natural Symbols* (1970), it is a well-observed feature of authoritarian codes that they dwell on bodily discipline, insisting on such things as short hair, closely-cut fingernails and rigorous personal hygiene. Get the body of the individual in line, and society will look after itself. As Margaret Thatcher said to Jimmy Young, 'It's very much better if we live in a clean and tidy society' – and cleanliness and tidiness are classic fundamentalist and authoritarian virtues. John Wesley, in his sermon 'On Dress', exhorted his congregation:

> Let it be observed, that slovenliness is no part of religion; that neither this nor any text of Scripture, condemns neatness of apparel. Certainly this is a duty, not a sin. 'Cleanliness is, indeed, next to godliness.'

The idea is extended in the next sentence of the address ... *instincts and convictions which I am convinced are far more deeply rooted than is often supposed.* The appeal to rootedness (q.v.), conviction (q.v.) and instinct is central to the Prime Minister's political philosophy. Within the body of a good – a clean and tidy – man are all the necessary lineaments of government and social organisation. If thou wouldst find God, or Government, search in thine own heart . . .

So it is inevitable that *the ties of the family which are at the heart of our society . . . are the very nursery of civic virtue.* 'Don't blame society – that's no one!' said Mrs Thatcher on *The Jimmy Young Programme.* The family, that little assembly of individual souls, pooling its roots, convictions and instincts, is the largest human unit on which her idea of a nation can be securely built. This is clearly a matter of theological belief, not of sociological observation. As anyone who saw Paul Watson's classic television documentary, *The Family,* will acknowledge, a society which tried to model itself on the average real family would turn out to be a desperate arrangement. We should have to live in a state of more or less permanent civil war, with generation against generation, sibling against sibling, parent against parent, with rare intermissions of sentimental making-up. The society we actually live in is remarkable (compared with, say, a Middle Eastern Islamic republic) for the amount of legislation, and the quantity of social work, required to deal with divorce, domestic violence and child abuse. Families in broadly 'Christian' societies are anthropologically notorious for their turbulence, precisely because they are so much smaller and less extended than their counterparts in Africa, Arabia or the Pacific.

... *worse than an infidel* ... Mrs Thatcher, here as elsewhere, is quoting the *Authorised Version*. Both the *Revised Version* and *The New English Bible* prefer the word 'unbeliever' to 'infidel', which has had a much more specific meaning in English since the time of the Crusades. It signified first an Assyrian, then any Muslim. It would be easy to overlook this piece of verbal tactlessness were it not for a passage, 250 words further on in the address, where Mrs Thatcher shows a remarkable scrupulosity in her choice of words to describe the relationship between Christianity and Judaism – even going to the extent of inventing an entirely new coinage. Given her care there, this use of *infidel* seems niggardly. Behind the word crouches the shadow of Christian England's oldest enemy, Islam – even as British Muslims now far outnumber practising English Methodists or practising Scottish Calvinists.

... *laws to provide for health and education, pensions for the elderly, succour for the sick and disabled* ... This is a minimum-terms agreement. The jobless, and the poor on bottom-line wages, together with families whose procreative powers have outstripped their economic ones, are firmly excluded from the list of people to whom society owes *sustenance*, *help* and *opportunity*. The word *succour* has a nicely Biblical ring; it also encodes a somewhat guarded promise. The sick should not so much be healed or, simply, cared for, as offered 'aid' or 'assistance', which is all *succour* means.

The next paragraph needs to be quoted in full, since it contains an original, and sophisticated, theory of sticks-and-carrots:

> . . . *intervention by the State must never become so great that it effectively removes personal responsibility. The same applies to taxation for while you and I would work extremely hard whatever the circumstances, there are undoubtedly some who would not unless the incentive was there.*
>
> *And we need* their *efforts too.*

So poor people who are lazy must be deprived of State money in order to drive them to work, while rich people who are lazy must be given more money by the State in order to persuade them to go on working. Both subsidies and tax-breaks are instruments for dealing with laziness in an impure, theologically unsound world. *You and I*, as co-religionists, co-fundamentalists, need neither – and nor would *they* if *they* shared *our* religious principles. Nowhere has the Prime Minister stated

55

her position on this important issue quite so clearly as she does here. The cynical view that she takes of her fellow citizens, both rich and poor, together with her polar methods for dealing with the laziness of the rich and the laziness of the poor, are expressed with a fierce certainty and concision.

There's an uncharacteristic pallidity in the section of the address devoted to the *proper* place of R. E. on the school curriculum, with its windy invocation of *heritage* and its frankly diplomatic enlistment of Sir Walter Scott, alongside Shakespeare, as an example of a writer whose work is illumined by an understanding of Christian history. In his biography of Mrs Thatcher, Patrick Cosgrave (who was a literary scholar and critic before entering politics as a commentator, then as a speech-writer) has a good deal to say about the Prime Minister's own reading. Neither Shakespeare nor Scott figures on the list. After Kipling, her favourite author is said to have been Richard Hillary (*The Last Enemy*), followed by J. B. Priestley, Howard Spring and A. P. Herbert.

Much the most interesting aspect of this section is her insistence that Judaism is the equal twin to Christianity in the national religious *heritage*. Three times she uses the phrase *Judaic–Christian tradition* (or *inheritance*). It is an expression of her own, without dictionary precedent. The conventional phrase is 'Judaeo-Christian', which turns Judaism into an adjective modifying the noun of Christianity. It suggests a continuum, in which Jewish history is absorbed into the later history of Christianity. *Judaic–Christian* gives both words exactly the same grammatical status. It can now be reversed, into *Christian–Judaic*, without changing its meaning or altering the weight given to the two components of the compound.

That equalisation is important. To take so much trouble to remind the Scottish presbyterians that their religion exists side by side with that of the Jews is typical of the delicacy and care with which the Prime Minister always speaks of Judaism. Her concern goes back a long way – at least to 1938, when, according to the Harris biography, Alfred Roberts and his wife took in a teenage Jewish refugee called Edith, who was a pen-friend of Margaret's older sister, Muriel, and who was sent out of Vienna after Hitler's *Anschluss* of Austria. Harris writes:

> Edith's account of the Nazi regime, and of the persecution of the Austrian Jews, made a deep impression on the thirteen-year-old Margaret, in which horror of repression and compassion for the Jews combined to produce in her a precocious awareness of the struggle for democracy in a world threatened by brutal dictatorship and aggressive anti-Semitism.

57

Later, in 1957, she was adopted as Conservative candidate in the safe seat of Finchley, which she won in 1959 and still represents. Harris again:

> A large part of the population of Finchley is Jewish, and some of the most stalwart Conservative supporters come from that sector. Mrs Thatcher has made many friendships among them, learned much from them, and it is partly out of this experience that she is regarded by them as the most pro-Zionist Prime Minister of the century.

The trouble is that the line between being 'pro-Zionist' and anti-Arab (even anti-Muslim) is fusewire-thin. Because of this, the earlier use of the word *infidel* instead of *unbeliever* seems revealingly negligent.

Yet *one of the great principles of our Judaic–Christian inheritance is tolerance.* This introduces another minimum-terms agreement for immigrants *with other faiths and cultures.* They have *always been welcomed in our land, assured of equality under the law, of proper respect, and of open friendship.* It is a charter to be interpreted a little cautiously, taking into account Mrs Thatcher's unusual emendation to the injunction to love your neighbour as yourself. Immigrants must, of course, live up to our standards.

Emphatic negatives always suggest that what is being denied may be what is really being asserted.

William Empson once memorably pointed out that if Keats needed to use four negatives in one line of his *Ode to Melancholy* ('No, no, go not to Lethe, neither twist/Wolf's-bane, tight-rooted, for its poisonous wine . . .'), he clearly wanted to go to Lethe very badly indeed. The same principle applies to *There is absolutely nothing incompatible between this and our desire to maintain the essence of our own identity* – which manages to insinuate that there may, indeed, be something incompatible about it. After all, having the occasional stranger about the house doesn't normally threaten the *essence* of the host's identity; so why is this strenuous repudiation necessary?

Harris records that, sometime before the 1979 election, Mrs Thatcher said on television, 'People are really rather afraid that this country might be rather swamped by people with a different culture'. He later went on to question her about what he took to be her subsequent 'modification' of that statement. She replied ('with vigour'):

I *never* modified it! I stood by it one hundred per cent. Some people have felt swamped by immigrants. They've seen the whole character of their neighbourhood change. I stood by that statement one hundred per cent. And continue to stand by it. Of *course* people can feel that they are being swamped. Small minorities can be absorbed – they

59

can be assets to the majority community – but, when a minority in a neighbourhood gets very large, people *do* feel swamped. They feel their whole way of life has changed.

So the *absolutely nothing incompatible* line adds a further amendment to the charter. Immigrants are welcome provided that they remain a controllable minority within a neighbourhood and prove themselves to be *assets to the majority*. Both the Patels of Bradford and the black Robertses of Brixton and Toxteth might reasonably feel that these terms jeopardised the essence of their own identities.

... a neat definition of democracy ... It's a measure of Mrs Thatcher's treatment of history as mere 'heritage' that she can adapt Lincoln's Gettysburg Address (never *speech*, as she puts it here) in much the same style as one might find a new use for the Victorian commode. When Lincoln went to Gettysburg to bury and commemorate the Union dead at a critical stage of the Civil War, he identified the Union cause with the cause of democracy itself – democracy threatened with extinction by the slave-based Confederacy. He said:

> ... that we here highly resolve that these dead shall not have died in vain – that this nation, under

God, shall have a new birth of freedom – and that
government of the people, by the people, for the
people, shall not perish from the earth.

This was not 'giving the world a neat definition of
democracy'. It was pointing to the brute injustice
of the rule of the South and to the unassailable
moral ascendancy of the North. If 'government of
the people, *etcet*' were to 'perish from the earth', it
would fall to a slavocracy, to a society based on the
idea that for Negroes there were no inalienable
rights.

Why should Mrs Thatcher try to belittle Lincoln?
For this is what she does. His *neat definition of
democracy which has since been widely and enthusiastically adopted* is made to sound like a motto in
a Christmas cracker. Its widespread adoption is
rendered subtly suspect by the word *enthusiastically*,
as if people had gone a bit over the top about it.
Enthusiasm is not a term of praise in the Nonconformist vocabulary; it suggests excess and delusion.
Wesley himself wrote: 'It is the believing those
to be Miracles which are not, that constitutes an
Enthusiast'. So democracy is 'one of those Miracles
which are not'?

    ... *what he enunciated as a form of government was
not in itself especially Christian* ... It was – and
crucially for the Northern cause – 'under God'. Its
specifically American history lay in those libertarian

and democratic aspects of Puritanism which had created the self-governing townships of New England. The Constitution defended by Lincoln was the joint product of a rigorous Christian tradition and eighteenth century Enlightenment thought, as practised by men like Jefferson and Franklin. That *nowhere in the Bible is the word democracy mentioned* is a very cheap red herring.

Lincoln, passionately championing a moral form of government in its darkest hour, is treated by Margaret Thatcher as if he was a fringe-bearded simpleton. The Gettysburg Address is used as a stick with which to beat something called *the mind of the majority*, a notion so far from Lincoln's own words and intentions that his presence here at all seems profoundly unnecessary, unless, of course, it was in Mrs Thatcher's mind that one great piece of political oratory should pay friendly, if condescending, salute to another.

. . . Nevertheless I am an enthusiast for democracy. The *nevertheless* turns the statement into a concession. The *enthusiast* hints that the concession may be a shade on the excessive side. The sentence sounds broadly cognate with 'Nevertheless I do have a weakness for liqueur chocolates'.

. . . not because I believe majority opinion is inevitably right or true, indeed no majority can take away God-given human rights. Mrs Thatcher evidently means that when a right is inalienable, it continues to exist

62

even when the freedom to exercise it is curtailed or taken away. Of course majorities (and minorities) can take away the exercise of *God-given human rights*, as the Confederate South had taken away the freedom of the Negroes to exercise their rights.

... *it most effectively safeguards the value of the individual* ... *Value* is a surprising word. 'Safeguards the individual' or 'safeguards the rights of the individual' must have been the phrases that first leaped to mind. Unless Mrs Thatcher means *value* in its economic sense, which seems unlikely, she must be attaching to the word a theological connotation and talking of man's *value* in the sight of God. Yet this is wholly inconsistent with her previous sentence, in which it was shown that an evil majority was incapable of taking away God-given rights. If that is so, how can a good government safeguard man's value before God?

And that is *a Christian concept.* Whenever Mrs Thatcher goes in for powerful rhetorical emphasis, one is inclined to smell a rat. There is nearly always something wrong with the logic of the overstressed sentence. Why is it a Christian concept? It could only be Christian if it were within the power of the state to protect *God-given human rights.* But it is not – or at least Mrs Thatcher has ringingly affirmed that it is not.

There was nothing *especially Christian* in Lincoln's 'definition' of government; there is something *especially Christian* in Mrs Thatcher's. Yet the words of the Gettysburg Address, read in their context, do claim the cause of the Union as a specifically Christian mission. Lincoln was fighting a holy war. As Julia Ward Howe put it in her 'Battle Hymn of the Republic':

As (Christ) died to make men holy, let us die
    to make men free,
While God is marching on . . .

Lincoln at Gettysburg was offering something far more explicitly Christian than anything said by Mrs Thatcher in Edinburgh. Though he was himself no more than a freethinker with mystical leanings, it was his triumph to identify the Union with the Will – and the Sacrifice – of God. By comparison with Lincoln, Mrs Thatcher's efforts to ally her government's cause with God's seem feeble.

We *Parliamentarians* . . . You *the Church* . . . In the final section of her address, Mrs Thatcher swings back to her opening antithesis, setting Parliament against the Church, law against faith, social reform against spiritual redemption. She pulls off a surprisingly good joke. *For, when all is said and done, a politician's role is a humble one.* The facetious echo of 'A policeman's lot is not a happy one' is aided and abetted by the internal rhyme of *done/one*. The flippancy of phrase is occasioned by the fact that, of course, the politician's role is not a humble one at all – a theme fantastically elaborated in Mrs Thatcher's discussion of Sir Cecil Spring-Rice's hymn, 'I vow to thee my country'.

Spring-Rice was the English Julia Ward Howe, and just as the Union troops marched to the 'Battle Hymn', so Kitchener's army went to the trenches inspirited by 'I vow to thee'. It is still a favourite among military men, much requested by retired colonels and generals in English parish churches. It has never been sung in the Church of Scotland.

It has only two stanzas. The first extols the glory of *pro patria mori*, crediting the soldiers with 'the love that pays the price . . . the love that makes undaunted the final sacrifice'. The second holds out the promise of eternal life after the unfortunate squaddie has met the bullet with his number on it.

It goes on to speak of 'another country I heard of long ago' . . . This is that same other country, from whose bourn no traveller returns, that so exercised Hamlet's thoughts. It is the country of the dead, or the Kingdom of Eternal Life. *'Soul by soul and silently her shining bounds increase.'* At Ypres, Verdun and on the Somme, the population of this other country was rising in direct proportion to the decrease in population of Britain, France and Germany.

There must be a good reason why Mrs Thatcher should want to end her address with this foreign hymn about young men dying. Perhaps it is intended to recall memories of her own triumph in the Falklands War, to bring back the stirring names of Darwin, San Carlos and Goose Green. To an English audience it would certainly have evoked the burial and thanksgiving services of the summer of '82, when the hymn itself was much in use. But the Scottish Presbyterians must have found this reference almost as baffling as Mrs Thatcher's earlier tribute to the splendours of ecclesiastical arts and crafts.

That, members of the Assembly, is the country which you chiefly serve. The line is like a bomb falling out of a clear sky. To the politicians, the living – and to the Church, the dead. It is a rhetorical gesture so extravagant and daring that one cannot believe that Mrs Thatcher means it. Certainly her last sentence, a limp one, suggests an imperfect comprehension of her preceding words. *Your success matters greatly – as much to the temporal as to the spiritual welfare of the nation. Success* is a watchword more often applied to industrial concerns than to churches, and one may guess that the whole sentence is a variant on a final line that has seen better days when delivered to the Confederation of British

Industry or the board of ICI. We are abruptly restored to the real world, whose ways are not the ways of gentleness and whose paths are not all paths of peace; to that first country, which Mrs Thatcher chiefly serves.

The speech was not much liked by the Assembly. The day after it was delivered, a senior Scottish theologian, Professor Duncan Forrester, responded coldly to it on Radio Forth. He took particular exception to Mrs Thatcher's use of the Spring-Rice hymn and the gloss that she gave the words 'soul by soul': *Not group by group or party by party or even church by church – but soul by soul – and each one counts.* The Church, Professor Forrester reminded her, had never countenanced the idea of an 'individualist's paradise'.

Yet no attack on its eccentric theology, its flawed logic, its mercilessly scant language can rob Mrs Thatcher's speech of the remarkable consistency of its vision. It is stamped throughout with her peculiar integrity, her plainspun way with big ideas, her scornful and impatient certitude. Hardly an aspect of life is left out of its ambit, and the aspects hang together as parts of a clearly articulated whole. If Britain under Mrs Thatcher's government feels like a nation in the throes of a zealous and puritanical Reformation, its old priests on the run, its icons smashed, its centres of learning under siege, its history rewritten in the mould of a stiff new

67

orthodoxy, then this address supplies a text, a Proclamation, from which the engine of Reform derives a lot of its continuing energy.

It is an audacious piece of work. This is the language of power, of parliamentary majority translated into unimpeded action and unimpeded words; a language bereft of concessions, as it is bereft of all the usual strategies of persuasive argument. When the Prime Minister tramples on the susceptibilities, traditions and customs of her Scottish audience, that is her forthrightness. When she fails to see the inherent paradox of the ideas she touches on, that is a measure of her conviction. These are looking-glass terms, in which historical ignorance turns into a kind of precious freedom, a dismal paucity of phrase is recast as vibrant simplicity and the inert cliché as a warrant of the homely common touch. In the looking-glass world, a striking absence of imagination becomes a useful precondition for assured political action.

This is the language that a lot of people like to hear. It answers intimately to a general impatience with difficult abstractions and with the rhetoric of patrician mystification in which government has so often been conducted. People warm to its fierceness, to its air of cutting the cackle and getting to the marrow of things. There is real power in a rhetoric pared down to concrete nouns and numbers that can be counted on the fingers of one hand:

it has the raw freshness of Hemingway ('Morality is what you feel good after; immorality is something you feel bad after') after an overdose of George Eliot.

It is very much the language of that idealised family which Mrs Thatcher likes to hold up as the microcosm of the nation. In this particular family, much pooh-poohing goes on around the breakfast table. *Education's all very well, but some people have got a bit too much education for their own good . . . The trouble with the media nowadays . . . Of course the immigrants have got their rights, but fair's fair . . .* So the voices go, ripe with indignant commonsense; and part of Mrs Thatcher's triumph as a national leader has come from the way she has restored the language of government to the language of the family breakfast table. The march of 'Thatcherism' has gone in step to the drumbeat of received family wisdom and received family apophthegms.

It's worth remembering that, between the Education Act of 1871 and Mrs Thatcher's accession in 1979, the drift of government was towards rescuing the individual from that language and that family. The late industrial world was too complex and intellectually demanding for anyone to comprehend it adequately in terms of Sunday School and Mother's Knee, and so Victorian values found practical expression in the foundation of civic libraries, schools, universities, institutes of adult education.

The BBC was created in the same spirit; so was the Open University. For 100 years, governments of every colour were committed to enlarging the language of citizenship. Now Mrs Thatcher's government is committed to closing it.

She is herself a product of that – essentially Victorian – system, with its stress on the liberal arts as necessary ingredients even in a scientific or technical education. In order to read Chemistry at Oxford (against the advice of her headmistress), she needed a School Certificate pass in Latin, which she mugged up from scratch in a year. Her own academic career, far from leading her to cherish doubleness, fine shades of meaning, complex ideas, seems only to have inspired in her a withering contempt for those 'airy-fairy concepts' on which churchmen and professors waste their days, and to have excited an atavistic enthusiasm for 'roots', 'instincts', and 'convictions'.

It is a narrow and exclusive dialect, this language in which we are now governed: it bolsters the sense of community enjoyed by those who use it and repels outsiders who aren't members of the family and in on the code. As a language, it has real integrity, precisely because it derives from the natural vocabulary, the social outlook, the settled habits of mind of one person, the Prime Minister herself. All the words fit, all the pieties and prejudices interlock. In its ceremonial, religiose form, as here, it has the unpleasant ring of a new and pertly unctuous thieves' slang.

References

In trying to follow Mrs Thatcher's train of thought, I have had recourse to the following sources:

Kenneth Harris, *Thatcher*, London 1988. (Weidenfeld & Nicolson)

Patrick Cosgrave, *Margaret Thatcher: a Tory and her Party*, London 1978. (Hutchinson)

G. R. Elton, *Reformation Europe 1517–1579*, London 1969. (Fontana)

Robert Louis Stevenson, *The Lantern Bearers & Other Essays*, (edited by Jeremy Treglown), London 1987. (Chatto & Windus)

Hugh Brogan, *The Pelican History of the United States*, London, 1986. (Penguin)

Garry Wills, *Inventing America: Jefferson's Declaration of Independence*, London 1978. (Athlone Press)

Anne Pagan (compiler), *God's Scotland? The Story of Scottish Christian Religion*, Edinburgh, 1988. (Mainstream)

Mary Douglas, *Natural Symbols: Explorations in Cosmology*, London 1970 (Barrie & Rockliff)

Transcript of *The Jimmy Young Programme*, BBC Radio 2, 27th July 1988.

Hansard, Vol. 121, Issue 1425 pp 356–359.

Fodor's Greece, London 1987. (Hodder & Stoughton)

I am grateful to Mrs Anne Davis of the Church of Scotland in Edinburgh and to my father, Canon Peter Raban, for their guidance on points of theology.

About the Author

JONATHAN RABAN was born in 1942. After spending four years as a university lecturer, he became a professional writer in 1969. His books include *Soft City*, *Arabia*, *Old Glory*, *Foreign Land*, *Coasting*, and *For Love and Money*. He is a regular reviewer for *The Observer* and a Fellow of the Royal Society of Literature.

CHATTO

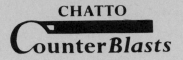

CounterBlasts

Also available in bookshops now:-

No. 2 Paul Foot   **Ireland: Why Britain Must Get Out**

No. 3 John Lloyd   **A Rational Advance for the Labour Party**

Forthcoming Chatto CounterBlasts

No. 4 Fay Weldon   **Sackcloth and Ashes, or The World on the Brink of Success**

No. 5 Peter Fuller   **Left High and Dry**

No. 6 Mary Warnock   **Universities: Knowing Our Minds**

No. 7 Sue Townsend   **Mr Bevan's Dream**

CounterBlasts to be published in 1990 include:-

Tessa Blackstone on prisons and penal reform
Christopher Hitchens on the Monarchy
Margaret Drabble on property and mortgage tax relief
Ruth Rendell & Colin Ward on decentralising Britain
Ronald Dworkin on a Bill of Rights for Britain
Adam Mars-Jones on Venus Envy
Robert Skidelsky on British education and the GCSE
Marina Warner on children and the 80s

plus pamphlets from Michael Holroyd, Hanif Kureishi, and Michael Ignatieff.

If you want to join in the debate, and if you want to know more about **CounterBlasts**, the writers and the issues, then write to:

Random House UK Ltd, Dept MH, Freepost 5066, London WC1B 3BR